Original adaption and Performances

Originally adapted for the radio and performed
by The Cleveland Radio Players. Directed by
Milton Matthew Horowitz. Recorded at Bad Racket
Studios.

Starring:

Denny Castiglione	The Voice of The Cleveland Radio Players
Eric Sever	Narrator
Logan Smith	Detective Chris Valentine
Dina Karalnik	Vanessa
Cory Shy	Captain Tellier
David Flynt	Officer 1
Andrew Jurcak	Officer 2
Jack Matuszewski	Evil Voice
Deanna Dionne	Operator

Killer Valentine

By

Milton Matthew Horowitz

CHRIS MYSTERY

CAST

                    NARRATOR
          monotone narrator with a bit of a
          chill to his voice

                    DETECTIVE CHRIS VALENTINE
          A detective working on a case that
          has run cold. He is agitated and,
          quite frankly, ready to give up.

                    VANESSA
          Detective Chris's late wife

                    CAPTAIN TELLIER
          the captain of the police force

                    OFFICER 1
          officer Cooper

                    OFFICER 2
          Officer Bradey

                    EVIL VOICE
          an ominous evil voice that harasses
          Detective Stery on the phone

                    OPERATOR
          the switchboard operator and police
          dispatcher

OPENING CREDITS

                    THE VOICE OF THE CLEVELAND RADIO PLAYERS
          Hello... This is the voice of The
          Cleveland Radio Players... My name
          is Denny Castiglione, ladies and
          gentlemen,

                                        OPENING FANFARE
          and you're listening to The
          Cleveland Radio Players performance
          of Killer Valentine Written and
          Directed by Milton Matthew
          Horowitz... Narrated by Eric Sever

ACT 1

DETECTIVE CHRIS STERY'S HOME

> NARRATOR
> It was particularly cold and
> blusterous Valentines day morning
> when our Detective, Chris Valentine
> woke up... the winter season had
> already felt like eternity since
> the last time Chris remembers a
> warm morning...

LIGHTING STOVE

POURING WATER

> NARRATOR
> Chis begins to brew himself some
> coffee... it's time like these
> Chris wishes he misses having a
> companion to share his cold
> mornings with... but then he
> remembers what happened the last
> woman he loved... and he vowed...
> never again...

FLASH BACK SFX

GUNSHOT ECHO

> VANESSA
> Chriiiissss!!!

FLASH BACK SFX

> NARRATOR
> reminded of his non-stop nightmare
> of a life Chris quickly shakes off
> the residue of his night terrors
> and beginnings brooding over case
> files

DRAWER OPENING

PAPER RUSTLING

> CHRIS
> It doesn't Make any sense Casper...
> why does this case still seem to
> allude me?

> NARRATOR
> Chris speaks to the only partner
> he'll ever trust again, his
> cat Casper... Casper is platinum

                    NARRATOR
white and Chris imagines, that if
his cat could... would un-friend
all humans if he thought he could
survive on his own... knowing he
can't, Casper humors his human care
taker and perches upon the work
desk as if pouring over the case
files with the detective

                              CAT MEOW + PURRING

                    CHRIS
I mean... It's been exactly a year
since the first murder Casper and
I still haven't made an arrest...
the captain is gonna can me any day
now if I don't turn up some
results... I think the only reason
he left me on the case is
because the first victim was...
well... you know who it was...

                              COFFEE PURCULATING

                    NARRATOR
just then the coffee Chris was
brewing finishes, he saunters to
the kitchen and pours himself a mug
of the crude like elixir and shifts
his attention back to the case
files...

                    CHRIS
all these suspects have gone cold
Casper... what am I going to do?
how am I going to serve justice to
the victims and to... Vanessa

                    NARRATOR
Vanessa was Chris's Late wife...
she was killed in an unsolved
homicide... its been a year this
very day since her death... and not
only does Chris feel like a failure
for not apprehending a culprit
yet... but he feels like hes failed
his late wife...

                    CHRIS
I'm running out of time Casper... I
feel like if I don't solve this
case soon... I may go mad... I feel

                    CHRIS
like I have been slipping...
Delious?... I don't know maybe...
this case is going to consume my
soul...Oh I'm sorry Casper I forget
to feed you?

                              CAT FOOD SFX

                    NARRATOR
the detective grabs a near by bag
of cat food and bends over to pour
it into Caspers bowl... only thing
is... the bowl, well its still full
of cat food... when is the last
time Detective Valentine fed his
dear cat?

                    CHRIS
Casper... you haven't been eating
lately... I'm starting to worry
about you buddy...

                    PHONE RING

                              SLOW MOTION FX

                    NARRATOR
the phone ring shatters the
silence... ... in slow motions
Chris drops his detective serum on
the floor

                         GLASS BREAK + SPILL

                    CHRIS
who could that be calling at five
A.M.?...

                              PHONE RING

                    CHRIS
Hello... Hello...

                    EVIL VOICE
Still working on the case
detective?

                              CUE EERIE MUSIC

                    CHRIS
who is this?

                    EVIL VOICE
ah ha... ha ha ha ha ha

                    CHRIS
who is this!....

                    EVIL VOICE
do you think your wife is at rest
considering your still a failure?

                    CHRIS
Listen here, when I find you, you
son of a

                    EVIL VOICE
please detective... spare me your
non-intimidating delusions of
grandeur... if you haven't even
solved one of the murders by now
then what makes you think I fear
you solving any of them?

                    CHRIS
Because I'm Detective Chris
Valentine and that's what I do, I
catch killers like you... just
because I haven't caught you yet
doesn't mean I've given up... and
any day now I'm gonna make an
arrest that you'll be on the other
end of my cuffs...

                    EVIL VOICE
ah ha... ah hahahahahahah

                              PHONE CLICK HANGING UP

                    NARRATOR
the voice on the other end of the
phone abruptly ends, sending chills
down our detectives spine... he
quickly thinks maybe he can get the
operator to trace the call lending
a new clue to a case that has gone
cold but then suddenly

                              PHONE RINGS AGAIN

                    CHRIS
look here you monster you don't
intimidate me and you better watch
your back because I'm coming for
you and when I catch you, your own

                    CHRIS
mother wont even recognize your
sorry mug

                    CAPTAIN TELLIER
Chris? who do you think your
talking to like that

                    CHRIS
oh captain... I'm sorry I thought
you were someone else...

                    CAPTAIN TELLIER
look Chris I think this case is
starting to take a toll on your
psyche...

                    CHRIS
I assure you captain I'm fine...
never better in fact

                    CAPTAIN TELLIER
well I hope you are... because we
have another one

                    CHRIS
what?

                    CAPTAIN TELLIER
that's right theres been another
murder... look get yourself
together and meet me 1025 Rose
Bulavard... you'll know your there
when you see the caution tape and
flashing Red lights...

                    CHRIS
1025 Rose Boulevard... got it...
see you there captain

                PHONE HANGS UP

                                        KEYS JINGLE

            CHRIS
don't wait up for me Casper

                FAST FOOTSTEPS
                        DOOR CLOSING + LOCKING

DRIVING

> NARRATOR
> as Chris rushes out the door he
> thinks to himself, this could be
> it... this could be the one to help
> crack the case wide open... maybe
> this time he made a mistake, he
> could have left some evidence or a
> clue that will lead to unveiling
> his identity... he keeps as calm as
> he can while driving to the scene
> of the crime

> TIRES SCREECHING

> NARRATOR
> even though his blood is boiling
> with anticipation Chris manages to
> safely drive himself to the scene
> of the crime... when he pulls up
> all excitement leaves his face as
> he pulls up to a home he recognizes
> as his former partners house
> decorated in caution tape and
> flashing police lights... out front
> of the home is a circus of forensic
> work choreographed around 2 crying
> children he knows to be his old
> partners kids, sobbing on what
> looks like a child protective
> service officer... Chris avoids eye
> contact with the children and and
> walks straight past the agent and
> through the front door, under some
> caution tape... he is quickly
> greeted by captain Tellier

CRIME SCENE

> CAPTAIN TELLIER
> Detective Valentine... thank you
> for getting here so quickly... I am
> very sorry that I had to contact
> you on today of all days...

> CHRIS
> it's just part of my job captain...
> what are we looking at here...

> CAPTAIN TELLIER
> well as you can tell were at Jims
> house... your old partner... there

CAPTAIN TELLIER
just through there near the sliding
glass door in the back...

CHRIS
don't tell me he killed them the
same way... is shes been cut ear to
ear and her wrists have been slit
vertically?

CAPTAIN TELLIER
the coroners looking at her now...
says it doesnt fit the other
murders its not ritualistic in
nature, and it wasnt done with
surgical precision... unless you
consdier a police issued
Nine-millameter a surgical
intrumnet... the Killer Valentine
is dead... he's in there on the
floor

CHRIS
Dont call him that... My name is
Valentine and I'm no killer... and
what do you mean its not like the
others... Guns? he never used
guns... what makes you think this
case is even related?

CAPTAIN TELLIER
well theres one thing different
this time

CHRIS
whats that?

CAPTAIN TELLIER
the killer left a message...

CHRIS
what?... where?

CAPTAIN TELLIER
it's just through there go ahead
have a look for yourself

ERRIE MUSIC

NARRATOR
our Detective walks under another
layer of caution tape to the heart
of the crime scene, various cops

                    NARRATOR
and other detective types litter
the room while a white haired
coroner hovers over the bodies of
two freshly slain individuals that
look a lot like his old partner and
his wife... Jim was his partner but
now hes just a statistic... his
body littered with gun holes, the
place torn apart in some sort of
struggle and his wife with a single
self inflicted gun wound to the
head.... it's when Chris looks down
at the bodies trails of blood
leading from their vitals that he
begins to have a flash back to his
own living nightmare

                              FLASHBACK SFX

                    VANESSA
Chris... Chris... help me.... help
me Chris I cant breath... he's
gonna kill me.... Chrisssss

                         GUNSHOT SFX ECHOS

                    CHRIS
you get your dam hands off of her!

                         CUT MUSIC AND FX

                    CAPTAIN TELLIER
Relax Detective... shes already
dead... the coroner is just trying
to calculate an accurate time of
death

                    NARRATOR
the Detective looms over the body
staring daggers at the coroner as
he makes his assessment of the
homicide... Chris slams back to
reality hard and begins to
apologize

                    CHRIS
I'm really sorry I didn't mean
it... I just...

                    CAPTAIN TELLIER
been working too hard... yeah I
briefed em all... look Detective I

                    CAPTAIN TELLIER
wanted to bring you hear to see
this homicide so that it might
bring some closure to this case for
you...

                    CHRIS
what do you mean? the killer is
still out there, there is no way
this case is related

                    CAPTAIN TELLIER
... not exactly

                    CHRIS
I'm sorry captain I don't
understand

                    CAPTAIN TELLIER
the killer left you a message this
time...

                    CHRIS
where?... I looked around the scene
I don't see any cryptic messages
or, any obvious messages written in
blood ... nothin like that

                    CAPTAIN TELLIER
it's here... it's all here in this
letter... written by the last
victim herself...

                    CHRIS
what... that cant be let me see
that

                              PAPER RUSTLE

                    NARRATOR
to our detectives surprise the
captain hands over a typed letter
with high velocity blood splatter
streaming down it... it's hard to
believe this note was left by the
killers... he's never left a note
and has killed 12 women now this
year... why leave a note now... the
detective begins to read the
letter... but as his late wife was
once a victim of this killer he can
only hear the voice of his late
wife vanessa

                    VANESSA
to whom it may concern, and my
loving family... I can no longer
live with the secret that I have
been hiding for the last year, I
regret to inform you all that my
husband is the one behind the 11
other killings that have terrorized
this local community... it all
started when he killed his partners
wife... somthing happened between
them that shouldn't have one night
and my husband sexually assaulted
and killed her... thing I overheard
my husband talking on the phone to
some other woman and I started
getting suspicious... I was in a
jealous rage at first I thought he
was just cheating, but when I found
out what was really going on I was
in disbelief, I was afraid for my
own life and didn't know what to
do... I thought it was a one time
thing... but then it kept
happening... I thought maybe most
of the other killings were to throw
the police off the investigation of
Detective Valentines wife... When I
finally confronted him he said that
picked most of the victims by
looking into their moral
shortcomings... said they were all
whores and sluts and that they were
evil people and deserved to die...
I wanted to believe him but yet I
still feel guilty for the crimes
and can no longer live with what I
have let my marriage become... I'm
sorry for the stress I may have
caused and feel the only way I can
make amends is by sentencing myself
to death, may God have mercy on my
soul...

                    NARRATOR
shocked by the letter the Detective
hands the letter back to the
captain...

                    CHRIS
did you have this letter checked
for fingerprints yet?

                    CAPTAIN TELLIER
of course we did detective even
though this is an apparent suicide
it's still being treated as a
homicide till we find other
evidence....

                    CHRIS
how do you know she wrote the
letter?

                    CAPTAIN TELLIER
there's no sign of forced entry and
the computer it was printed from is
right here... she was the only one
that had the password...

                    CHRIS
what about the husband?

                    CAPTAIN TELLIER
you mean your old partner, the guy
on the floor with six shots in him?
yeah we checked him out Detective,
It seems like everything she said
was true... we found files on his
computer... turns out he liked to
take pictures of himself... like
some sort of sick selfie fetish...
It's all going into the report...
which I don't suggest you read...

                    CHRIS
Did he take Pictures of my wife?

                    CAPTAIN TELLIER
Detective...

                    CHRIS
!! tell me right now Capetian does
he have pictures of my wifes Murder
!!

                    CAPTAIN TELLIER
calm down detective...

                    CHRIS
He does doesn't he! let me see
em... you son of a--

                                    KICK AND THUD

                    NARRATOR
just then the Detected kicks the
dead corpse of his former partner
in the head

                CAPTAIN TELLIER
dammit Valentine... Get him out of
here... you can't come in here and
start kicking our evidence around
in the head... just because you
don't like the outcome of this
case...

                    CHRIS
doesn't seem like the kind of
domestic dispute that would happen
between those two in front of their
children... I want those children
questioned by our personality
profilers...

                CAPTAIN TELLIER
detective those kids have been
through enough tonight I'm not
going to make it any worse for them
if I don't have to

                    CHRIS
those kids might hold the answer to
ending this investigation...

                CAPTAIN TELLIER
this investigation is over
detective... the killer is laying
here in the floor with a freshly
typed confession I think it's time
to consider this case closed

                    CHRIS
but captain

                CAPTAIN TELLIER
but nothing detective... look I'm
sorry this is the way you had to
find out about your wifes killer
but I figured I would let you see
first hand so we can put this to
rest once for all... and now I
suggest you do the same... go
home... punch out for the first
time in months... and get some
rest... Vanessa would want it this
way...

                    CHRIS
you haven't heard the last of this
captain

                    CAPTAIN TELLIER
oh yes I have... and if you bring
it up or I find out your still
working on this closed case ill
have you suspended indefinitely
without pay... now punch out
detective... that's an order...

                              FADE OUT CRIME SCENE

DRIVING

                              CUE UNSETTLING MUSIC

                    NARRATOR
and with that the detective left
the crime scene in angst... he
shuffled to his car in a trance and
begins to drive... to where he
doesn't know... but the shock of
the last crime scene puts him on
edge... could she really have
committed all those murders? how
could she slip through her
fingers... whats the connection of
the crimes... surely this cant be
the end of this case... wheres the
justice for the other victims...
where the justice for his wife? all
these questions fill up the mind of
our detective and before he knows
it he's sitting in his own driveway
looking at his neglected home from
the cold concrete... whats to go in
there for anymore... the case is
over... there will be no more
homicides... just then a daunting
thought entered his mind

                    CHRIS
but wait... what about the
caller... the caller was definitely
and was definitely not my old
partner... this case is not over...
not by a long shot...

DETECTIVE CHRIS STERY'S HOME

CAR DOOR SLAMS SHUT

FOOTSTEPS

            NARRATOR
lost and confused the detective
decides go back over his case files
one last time, but when he gets to
the door he notices something
disturbing

ERIE MUSIC RISING

            NARRATOR
the detective takes his keys out of
his pocket and tries to unlock the
door...

KEYS JINGLEING

            NARRATOR
but when he tries to push his key
in the lock, the door slowly creeks
open...

CREAKING DOOR

            NARRATOR
the detectives mind begins to
race... did he forget to lock his
door...

            CHRIS
Hello?... Hello is someone here?

            NARRATOR
was there an intruder during his
absence?... suddenly he notices
steaks of blood on the floor

            CHRIS
oh my God... Hello?!... whos in
there?

            NARRATOR
following the trail of blood
through his home he notices more
and more blood pooling towards his
study where he keeps his case
files...

                    CHRIS
my name is detective Chris
Valentine if anyone is in here I
suggest you come out with your
hands up... I have a gun and I have
deadly accuracy, now show
yourself!...

                    NARRATOR
there is no answer just the creepy
absence of sound in the modest
home... making his way to his study
the detective kicks open the

                              DOOR KICKING IN

                    CHRIS
oh no! ... Casper!

                    NARRATOR
upon flinging open the door the
detective discovers the dead body
of cat Casper hanging from the
ceiling fan with its neck slit and
its limbs lacerated from its
body... blood pools on the floor
below while the shaking of the fan
blades splatter blood in a circular
formation around the room...
noticing his case files are strung
around the room the vision is one
of utter shock and horror...

                    CHRIS
what sicko could have done this to
you Casper?... my files... my
pictures!

                              PHONE RING

                    NARRATOR
the phone rings sending a chill
down the detectives spine again...
he quickly picks it up before it
can ring again

                              PHONE PICK UP

                    CHRIS
Hello....

                    EVIL VOICE
Hello detective... did you get my
Valentines Day present?

                    CHRIS
who is this?

                    EVIL VOICE
hahahhaha oh you... you know I cant
tell you that... it would take all
the sport out of the game

                    CHRIS
this isn't a game you sick
psychopath... I might be sworn to
uphold and protect the laws but you
cant fool me like the rest of the
prescient... when I find out who
you are... I'm gonna kill you

                    EVIL VOICE
oh ho ho ho... but you do have to
find me first now don't you...
don't get ahead of yourself
detective... this is far from
over... hahahahahaha

              PHONE CLICKS OFF

                              HANGS UP PHONE

                    NARRATOR
spooked by the caller once more the
detective looks around his horrific
blood splattered study before
having an epiphany

                    CHRIS
wait a minute...

              PICKS UP PHONE

                              DIAL TONE

                    NARRATOR
the detective picks up the phone
and dials the operator

                    OPERATOR
Hello you've reached the operator
how can I direct your call?

                    CHRIS
hello this is detective Chris
Valentine and I need the last phone
number to dial my line

                    OPERATOR
please hold...(long pause)... the
last number that dial this line was
555-1234

                    CHRIS
555-1234? are you sure miss that
can't be correct

                    OPERATOR
yes sir I'm positive

                    CHRIS
but that's the line to the police
station?

                    OPERATOR
I'm sorry sir but I have to keep
this line clear if there's no
further inquires I'm going to
disconnect you now...

                    NARRATOR
Disconnecting the detective from
the phone was the least of Chris's
worries...the calls were coming
from the police station... Chris
stood there speechless holding the
now dead phone to his head staring
and his beloved dead cat... trying
to piece together the fragments of
the facts he's just heard...
puzzled he hangs up the phone

                PHONE CLICK

                                        PHONE RING

                    NARRATOR
the phone rings again instantly and
without thinking he picks it right
back up

                    CHRIS
Hello...

                    CAPTAIN TELLIER
Detective...

                    CHRIS
yes captain?...

CAPTAIN TELLIER
listen I'm gonna go ahead and have
you to come in and bring all your
work on the recent string of
murders... now that the case is
close were going to have to
disclose everything to internal
affairs...

CHRIS
yes captain...

CAPTAIN TELLIER
are you ok?

CHRIS
yes captain... Ill be there right
away...

PHONE HANGS UP

NARRATOR
numb with confusion our detective
stares off in to space with a
hollow look in his eyes... and a
surreal voice he speaks out

CHRIS
(monotone)
did ya hear that Casper? we solved
the case... It's finally closed
now... let's take the captain our
paper work and show him what a good
job I did on this case...

NARRATOR
in a Thorazine like shuffle the
detective begins grabbing all his
paperwork and pictures and starts
compiling them in to one giant
folder covered in the blood
splatter from the hanging cat in
the middle of the room...
acknowledging the cat again the
detective says

CHRIS
(monotone)
Ok Casper I'm off to the police
station now... don't wait up for
me...

                    NARRATOR
leaving his recently killed cat
still wobbling from the shaky
ceiling fan the detective grabs his
keys and exits the home

                 KEYS JINGLE
                 DOOR SHUTS
                                    SLOW FOOTSTEPS

DRIVING

                    NARRATOR
the detective saunters out to his
car and in a zombie like haze
begins to drive himself to the
police station...

                         CAR STARTS + DRIVES AWAY

                    NARRATOR
he pulls out of the drive way and
begins his long cold drive to the
police station when suddenly he
notices a pair of headlights pull
up behind him, he does nothing to
shield his eyes from the glare...
it's as if hes been iced over with
so much stress and violence that
his unflinching eyes still remain
focused down the road...

                                    TIRE SCREECH

                    NARRATOR
he takes a turn at high speed
skidding in the wet snowy street...
the car behind him remains close
behind

                                    TIRE SCREECH

                    NARRATOR
again the detective whips the car
around a turn slipping and
squealing around the bend... the
car behind him is still close
behind so close in fact the
detective can start to make out
that it's a police cruiser that's
been hot on his trail... and just
then the flashers come on followed
by siren

                              POLICE SIREN

                NARRATOR
the detective pulls over to the
side of the road real casual like

                  CAR PULLS OVER
                              CUT POLICE SIRENS

                NARRATOR
an office in uniform steps out of
the cruiser and slowly marches
towards the detectives door...

                3 TAPS ON GLASS
                    WINDOW MANUALY ROLLING DOWN

                CHRIS
what seems to be the problem
officer?

                OFFICER 1
Detective Valentine? is that you

                CHRIS
yes officer

                OFFICER 1
uh yea the reason I pulled ya over
is you were haulin' ass through
some of those turns and I think ya
missed a stop sign or two... Is
there something you wanna tell me

                CHRIS
no office... everything's fine... I
was just on my way to see the
captain...

                NARRATOR
just then Detective Valentine
begins to get paranoid that the
officer notices the files in the
passenger seat spattered with
blood... on closer inspection so is
the detectives hands...

                OFFICER 1
I hate to do this to you Detective
but do you mind stepping out of the
car for a second?

                    CHRIS
I'm really sorry to have to do this
officer...

                    OFFICER 1
keep your hands where I can see
them!

                              2 GUNSHOTS IN QUICK SUCCESSION

                    NARRATOR
the detective draws first and
double taps the office with 2
bullets putting him down

                              CAR STARTS + DRIVES AWAY

                    NARRATOR
the detective fleas the scene while
the 2nd office in the patrol car
rushes over the the fallen officer
while grabbing his police radio and
speaking the jargon

                              RADIO SQUELCH

                    OFFICER 2
this is officer Bradey I with
officer cooper and he's been
shot... I have an officer down... I
repeat, officer down...

                    OPPERATOR
10-4 officer down... whats your 20
officer Bradey?

                    OFFICER 2
I'm 3 blocks east of Rose on
Ridgeburry...

                    OPPERATOR
on ridgeburry didn't you just call
for a plate check?

                    OPPERATOR
yeah officer Cooper just did

                    OPPERATOR
it just came back to a Vanessa and
Chris Valentine...

                    OFFICER 2
Detective Valentine? ... oh man hes
finally snapped... is the captain
there? can you put me through to
him?

                    OPPERATOR
please hold...

                    CAPTAIN TELLIER
Bradey? whats happened to Cooper?

                    OFFICER 2
It was Detective Valentine sir...
he shot Cooper twice and drove off

                    CAPTAIN TELLIER
but I just talked to Valentine 5
minutes ago... Listen you stay with
Cooper til EMS arrives we'll take
care of Detective Valentine...

                    OFFICER 2
Rodger that stay with Cooper til
EMS arrives... oh and captain... be
careful I think Valentines is
headed your way...

                                        RADIO SQUELCH

                    NARRATOR
be careful indeed captain Tellier,
because right on its way to you is
a man so unstable from his own
delusions that his natural paranoia
began to get the best of him and
unravel him at the seems

                                        DRIVING SOUNDS

                    CHRIS
        (v.o.)
how could I have been so stupid? of
course the Evil voice was none
other then captain Tellier... I
wondered how he would always manage
to call right after the killer
would taunt me... and the letter, I
knew it was a fake... the captain
must have got to the crime scene
first and planted the letter... I
bet he thought her confession would
cover up all the murders... but

                    CHRIS
why... why so many girls? did the
captain kill them all? ... did he
Kill Vanessa?

                    NARRATOR
racing through his mind are all the
sick twisted scenarios that the
murders could have been carried out
in... he frantically tries to make
sense of it all but he just can't
his anger consumes his mind and
drives him mad with rage, suddenly
he starts to see red!... has he
gone over the edge he asks himself?
no its just more police cruisers on
his tail... he takes a sharp
unexpected turn

                 TIRES SQUEALING

                                        CAR CRASH

                    NARRATOR
Wham!... two police cruisers
collide with one another trying to
keep up with the Detectives quick
moves... he skids around another
turn hammering down the throttle

                                        CAR SPEEDING

                    NARRATOR
pretty soon his target comes into
view... it's the police station...
bearing down the small building the
detective put his foot to the floor
and but for a moment his mind is
clear... and he can almost hear
angles sing... and just as a
heavenly tear would burst forth

                                        LARGE SMASH

                    NARRATOR
the detectives car hops the curb
and explodes though the front
facade of the police station...
cruisers in pursuit finally catch
up

              POLICE SIRENS ARRIVE THEN CUT OFF

                    NARRATOR
          the detective quickly grabs for his
          gun and springs from the
          wreckage... other police near by
          can see him emerging from the
          rubble and begin to hail gunfire at
          him

                                        GUNFIRE

THE POLICE STATION

                    NARRATOR
          meanwhile inside the police station
          the captain and a few of his best
          men were waiting inside with heavy
          fire power

                    CAPTAIN TELLIER
          good god men I think he drove
          through the front wall... heads up
          watch each others backs...

                    NARRATOR
          the 3 police office begin to march
          down the halls of the prison in a
          military raid style, one high...
          one low... and the captain
          following close behind... then they
          hear the sound of gunshots

                                        2 GUNSHOTS

                    NARRATOR
          a familiar voice call out

                            CUE SUSPENSEFUL CREEPY MUSIC

                    CHRIS
          captain... I bet you didn't think I
          would figure it out...

                    CAPTAIN TELLIER
          Detective Valentine... I'm gonna
          have to ask you to stand down...
          your behavior as a detective is
          unacceptable... put down your
          weapons and come out...

                    CHRIS
          Oh you'd like that wouldn't you...
          that way no one would every learn
          about all those murders you tried
          to cover up...

                    CAPTAIN TELLIER
I don't know what our talking about
Detective

                              PAPER SPLAHING ON THE FLOOR

          NARRATOR
just then from the shadows a manila
envelope splahes into the hallway
littering the floor with crime
scene photos of the recent string
of murders

          CAPTAIN TELLIER
listen whatever you're thinking
Detective... It's a bad idea...
just surrender peacefully and we
can talk all this out...

                    CHRIS
It's a little late for that
captain... I've already killed a
few of your henchmen you think im
gonna stop now?... after what you
did!... All those girls!... my Wife
Vanessa!

          CAPTAIN TELLIER
I should have taken you off this
case months ago... it's my own
fault and for that I'm sorry... but
this isn't the answer

          NARRATOR
just then the detective springs out
into the dark hallway and busts off
a couple of hip shot

                    2 GUNSHOTS + RANDOM GUNSHOTS

          NARRATOR
2 of the officers are hit but
manage to return fire... the
Captain can barely see through the
dark smoke filled prison
hallways... the downed officers
begin to moan in the dark

                              OFFICERS MOANING

          NARRATOR
just then the sounds of other
officers come flooding in through

                    NARRATOR
the back hall and they spot the
detective crawling towards his
gun...

                    CAPTAIN TELLIER
Be careful he's got a gun... crazy
bastard shot us all up...

                    NARRATOR
one of the officers quickly shoots
the detective with a taser gun

                                        TASER SOUNDS

                    NARRATOR
the detective is quickly overrun
with officers they pry his arms
behind his back and they all take
turns putting their knees in his
neck as he flop on the ground like
an electrified fish...

                    CAPTAIN TELLIER
take him to a cell and have him
restrained until we can get a head
doctor to take a look at him... get
cozy Detective Valentine your gonna
be there a while...

                                        STRUGLING SFX

                    CHRIS
you'll never get away with this...
ya hear me captain! NEVER!... I'm
the greatest detective that ever
lived my name is Chris Valentine...
Chris Valentine! ... It's
Valentines day!... you gotta listen
to me boys... trace the phone
calls... go to my house, he hung my
cat... he killed my Cat! my poor
Casper... ya gotta believe me
fella... I couldn't make this kind
of thing up...

                                        CONCLUSION MUSIC

                    NARRATOR
however the Killer Detective
Valentine, or Killer Valentine as
he would come to be known would
never solve the puzzeling string of

                    NARRATOR
murders that started on Valentines
day with his wife... and hes
probably looking at consecutive
life sentences... the detective
Chris Valentine let his natural
paranoia become his obsession...
during the court case it came out
that there was no Evil caller and
the detective never even owned a
cat... he stood trial a few months
after his arrest so that the
prosecution could built up a
case... he was ultimately charged
with the murder of three police
officers and attempted vehicular
homicide on another two cops... the
papers tried to explain it as work
place grievances but in the end
everyone close to the case knew
that the detective when mad from
unsolved case file after unsolved
case file... the only true mystery
here is what was real and what was
in Detective Chris Valentines
head... he sat in Maximum security
prision for almost a year without a
single visitor until one day...
Valentines day to be exact... 2
years after his wifes death... a
gaurd comes to his cell door and
says

                    OFFICER 1
Valentine... you have a phone
call...

                    NARRATOR
escorted down the hall to a small
cubical with nothing but a phone in
it... the former Detective now
prisioner picks up the phone

                    CHRIS
Hello...?

                    EVIL VOICE
Happy Valentines Day Detective...
ha ha ha ha ha hahahahah

                    PHONE CLICK

                                        FADE OUT

END CREDITS

FADE IN CREDITS THEME

THE VOICE OF THE CLEVELAND RADIO PLAYERS
You have been listening to The
Cleveland Radio Players performance
of Killer Valentine... Written and
Directed by Milton Matthew
Horowitz... Starring...

And my name is Denny Castiglione
Ladies and Gentleman... Killer
Valentine was recorded live at Bad
Racket Studios... Copyright 2016.

Rights and Royalties

Originally adapted for the radio and performed
by The Cleveland Radio Players

Directed by Milton Matthew Horowitz

Recorded at Bad Racket Studios

For more information on performance rights and
royalties, or to listen to Killer Valentine as
a radio play, please visit
www.ClevelandRadioPlayers.com

www.ingramcontent.com/pod-product-compliance
Lightning Source LLC
Chambersburg PA
CBHW081234020426
42331CB00012B/3167